Date: 8/22/19

Write It Right

Writing a Book Report

By Cecilia Minden and Kate Roth

Published in the United States of America by
Cherry Lake Publishing
Ann Arbor, Michigan
www.cherrylakepublishing.com

Reading Adviser: Marla Conn MS, Ed., Literacy specialist, Read-Ability, Inc.
Book Designer: Felicia Macheske
Character Illustrator: Carol Herring

Photo Credits: © Africa Studio/Shutterstock.com, 5; © Sleeping Bear Press, 7; © wavebreakmedia/Shutterstock.com, 13; © Edward Lara/Shutterstock.com, 15; © Oleg Troino/Shutterstock.com, 19

Graphics Throughout: © simple surface/Shutterstock.com; © Mix3r/Shutterstock.com; © Artefficient/Shutterstock.com; © lemony/Shutterstock.com; © Svetolk/Shutterstock.com; © EV-DA/Shutterstock.com; © briddy/Shutterstock.com; © IreneArt/Shutterstock.com

Library of Congress Cataloging-in-Publication Data

Names: Minden, Cecilia, author. | Roth, Kate, author. | Herring, Carol, illustrator.
Title: Writing a book report / by Cecilia Minden and Kate Roth ;
[illustrator] Carol Herring.
Description: Ann Arbor, Michigan : Cherry Lake Publishing, [2019] | Series:
Write it right | Includes bibliographical references and index. |
Audience: K to Grade 3.
Identifiers: LCCN 2018034531| ISBN 9781534142831 (hardcover) | ISBN
9781534139398 (pbk.) | ISBN 9781534140592 (pdf) | ISBN 9781534141797
(hosted ebook)
Subjects: LCSH: Report writing—Juvenile literature. | Book
reviewing—Juvenile literature.
Classification: LCC LB1047.3 M56 2019 | DDC 372.62/3—dc23
LC record available at https://lccn.loc.gov/2018034531

Cherry Lake Publishing would like to acknowledge the work of The Partnership for 21st Century Skills.
Please visit *www.p21.org* for more information.

Printed in the United States of America
Corporate Graphics

Table of
CONTENTS

CHAPTER ONE

What a Good Book!

There are many kinds of books. Some are **fiction**. The events and **characters** in these books are not real. Writers make them up using their imaginations. There are also **nonfiction** books. These books are about real people and events. A **biography** is an example of nonfiction.

Sometimes, teachers ask students to read books and write reports. A book report is a way to tell others about a book you have read. Book reports have many parts. They explain what the book is about. They also include your **opinion** of the book. Let's work on writing a book report!

What kind of book do you like to read?

It takes practice to write a good book report.

CHAPTER TWO

Parts of a Book Report

Your book report should include the title and author of the book. Is there an **illustrator**? Include this person too.

Reports on fiction books should describe the **setting**, characters, and **plot**. The setting is where and when the story takes place. Characters are usually the people or animals in the book. The plot is what happens in the book. There often is a problem and **solution**.

Nonfiction book reports are a bit different. They describe the book's subject. The subject is the person or thing that is written about in a book. What's the subject of a book about the moon? The moon! The book report also includes facts from the book.

Nonfiction books are full of facts.

Can you find the title and author's name on this book cover?

Make a Chart

You've read your book. Now you need to organize your thoughts. A chart can help you do this. Look at the chart on page 9. It shows one way to map out the parts of a fiction book report. Now make a chart for your book.

HERE'S WHAT YOU'LL NEED:

- The book
- Notebook paper
- Ruler
- Pencil

INSTRUCTIONS:

1. Write your name and the date at the top of a sheet of paper.
2. Use a ruler to help you make the six boxes.
3. Do you see how the boxes in the chart on page 9 are labeled? Label your chart in the same way. Each box is for a different idea.
4. Fill in the boxes of your chart using information from your book. Leave the "My Opinion" box blank for now.

Sample Fiction Book Report Chart

NAME: Tristan Holland

DATE: 9/10/2019

TITLE: *Zacktastic*

AUTHOR: Courtney Sheinmel

ILLUSTRATOR: Jennifer A. Bell

CHARACTERS

Zack Cooley
Quinn Cooley (Zack's twin sister)
Uncle Max
Trey, Shaggy, and Buzz
Mr. Heddle/Linx

PLOT

Beginning: On Zack's 10th birthday, Uncle Max tells him that he comes from a long line of genies.

Middle: Zack is sent on his first assignment, even though he hasn't really learned how to be a genie.

End: Zack resolves the problem but has many narrow escapes.

SETTING

Zack's home
Uncle Max's home
Millings Academy

PROBLEM AND SOLUTION

Zack learns he is a genie. Zack succeeds at his first task.

MY OPINION

9

CHAPTER THREE

What Do You Think?

Have you ever read a book report? Did it help you decide if you wanted to read the book? Your opinion of a book is important. Share your ideas. Others will read your book report. It will help them decide if they would also like to read the book.

ACTIVITY

Go back to the chart you started earlier. It is time to fill in the "My Opinion" box.

INSTRUCTIONS:

Ask yourself these questions:
- Which characters did you like or not like? Why?
- What was the best part of the book?
- Are there pictures? Do they add to the story? How?
- Should others read this book? Why?
- Does this book remind you of another book you've read? Why?

Fill in the "My Opinion" box of your chart.
  Be sure to explain your opinions. Use information from the book to support and back up your ideas.

NAME: Tristan Holland

DATE: 9/10/2019

TITLE: *Zacktastic*

AUTHOR: Courtney Sheinmel

ILLUSTRATOR: Jennifer A. Bell

CHARACTERS

Zack Cooley
Quinn Cooley (Zack's twin sister)
Uncle Max
Trey, Shaggy, and Buzz
Mr. Heddle/Linx

PLOT

Beginning: On Zack's 10th birthday, Uncle Max tells him that he comes from a long line of genies.

Middle: Zack is sent on his first assignment, even though he hasn't really learned how to be a genie.

End: Zack resolves the problem but has many narrow escapes.

SETTING

Zack's home
Uncle Max's home
Millings Academy

PROBLEM AND SOLUTION

Zack learns he is a genie. Zack succeeds at his first task.

MY OPINION

I think this was a good book. Zack gets into some wild situations. While he doesn't always make the best choices, he tries hard to do the right thing. It was fun to imagine what I would do if I was a genie and then see if that matched Zack's choices.

CHAPTER FOUR

Nonfiction

Nonfiction book reports are written in a different way. You report on the facts you read in the book. You will also report on the **setup** of the book.

People are always looking for a good book. Share your ideas.

Nonfiction Chart

HERE'S WHAT YOU'LL NEED:

- The book
- Notebook paper
- Ruler
- Pencil

INSTRUCTIONS:

1. Write your name and the date at the top of a sheet of paper.
2. Turn to the chart on page 13. Use a ruler to help you make the 4 boxes.
3. Do you see how the chart's boxes are labeled? Label your chart in the same way.
4. Fill in your chart using information from your book.
   - What interesting facts did you learn?
   - Did the way the book was set up help you understand the facts?
   - Why did you pick this subject?

Sample Nonfiction Book Report Chart

NAME: Maria López   DATE: 6/19/18

TITLE: *Tell Me Why: The Moon Changes Shape*   AUTHOR: Kathryn Beaton

MAIN IDEAS
What is this book about? What are the main points and facts?
This book is about why the moon seems to change shapes during the month. There are phases of the moon where we can see a sliver and others where we see a full circle.

INTERESTING FACT
What is the most interesting fact you learned?
That there are thousands of big craters on the moon and there could be millions of smaller ones.

BOOK SETUP
How is the book set up? Are there different chapters for different ideas?
The book is divided into the phases of the moon. Nick and his grandmother talk about why the moon seems to change shape at each phase.

Is there an **index**? Does it help you find facts?
Yes. Yes.

Are there pictures? Do they help you understand the subject?
Yes. Yes.

MY OPINION
Does the book describe the subject in an interesting way? Why or why not?
Yes, because the author presents the information in the form of a conversation between Nick and his grandmother.

Did the book help you learn about the subject? Why or why not?

Yes, because the author gave clear explanations. The ideas are easy to understand.

Should others read this book? Why or why not?
Yes, because everyone should learn more about the moon.

Share what you learn with others!

CHAPTER FIVE

Writing a Book Report

Now it is time to write your book report. Take a look at these sample book reports before you begin.

Sample Nonfiction Book Report

NAME: Maria López   **DATE:** 6/19/18

Tell Me Why: The Moon Changes Shape is a great book. The author is Kathryn Beaton.

I enjoyed reading about the moon. The most interesting thing I learned was that there are thousands of big craters on the moon and there could be millions of smaller ones.

The book has four parts. Each part has information about the phases of the moon. I learned that while it seems the moon is changing shape, it is really the amount of sunlight we can see reflected from the moon.

The author writes this book as a conversation between Nick and his grandmother over the course of a month. I think this makes the information clear and easy to understand. Every other page has a photo to help with the explanations. There are also other facts and questions with answers about the moon.

This book is a good choice to read in class or for fun. Everyone should learn more about the phases of the moon!

NAME: Tristan Holland   DATE: 9/10/2019

I read *Zacktastic*, written by Courtney Sheinmel and illustrated by Jennifer A. Bell.

Uncle Max comes to a birthday party at Zack's home for Zack and his twin sister, Quinn. Uncle Max's present is a green bottle and a surprise announcement. Zack is a genie! Before Zack can think about what this means, he is whooshed through a portal to his first assignment at Millings Academy. He must save Trey from two bullies, Shaggy and Buzz.

Zack isn't sure what to do, but then his genie powers begin to kick in. Zack bumbles effort after effort but eventually figures out a plan. After Trey is safe and Zack thinks all is well, a more dangerous threat occurs in the form of Linx, an evil super genie. Linx is disguised as Mr. Heddle, the headmaster of the school.

Just when it seems all is lost, Uncle Max appears and helps Zack figure out how to get rid of Linx.

I enjoyed this book. It was fun to imagine what I would do if I was a genie and then see if that matched Zack's choices. You should read this book. Then you can find out how Zack survived his first genie assignment.

Putting It All Together

Now you are ready to write your book report.

HERE'S WHAT YOU'LL NEED:

- The book
- Pen
- Your chart
- Notebook paper
- Computer (if you want to type the report)

INSTRUCTIONS:

1. Write your name and the date at the top of the paper.
2. Write the title of the book and the name of the author in the first **paragraph** of your report.
3. Use the information in your chart to help you write your report.
4. Use examples or facts from the book to support your ideas.
4. Be sure to **indent** each new paragraph.

Your chart will help you remember what you want to write.

CHAPTER SIX

Editing

Good job! You've written or typed your report. Now you need to check your work.

It is important to edit your book report. Read the finished report out loud. This will help you find mistakes. Try it. Does a sentence sound too long? Did you spell the words correctly? Ask an adult to help you. This is the time to make changes to your report.

Try reading your work aloud to an adult. Ask them to listen for ways to make your report better.

Checking for Mistakes

Ask yourself these questions as you check your report:

- Did I remember that fiction and nonfiction reports cover different ideas?
- Did I complete the correct chart for the type of book I read?
- Did I use my chart as a guide as I wrote?
- Did I write my name and the date?
- Did I indent my paragraphs?
- Did I leave a space between paragraphs?
- Did I make my ideas clear?
- Did I spell all my words correctly?

Now you know how to write an interesting book report. Which book will you read next?

GLOSSARY

biography (bye-AH-gruh-fee) a person's life story, which is usually written down

characters (KAR-ik-turz) the people or animals in a story

fiction (FIK-shuhn) writing that tells made-up stories

illustrator (IL-uh-stray-tur) a person who creates pictures for books

indent (in-DENT) to start a line of writing farther in from the left edge of a page than the other lines

index (IN-deks) a list of subjects and the pages where they appear in a book

nonfiction (nahn-FIK-shuhn) writing that is about real events, people, or things

opinion (uh-PIN-yuhn) a person's beliefs and ideas about somebody or something

paragraph (PAIR-uh-graf) a group of sentences about certain ideas or subjects

plot (PLAHT) the main story or order of events in a book

setting (SET-ing) the time and place of the action in a story

setup (SET-uhp) the way that something is arranged

solution (suh-LOO-shuhn) an explanation of or answer to a problem

BOOKS

Faundez, Anne. *How to Write Reports*. Laguna Hills, CA: QEB Publishing, Inc., 2007.

WEBSITES

KidsHealth—How to Pick a Great Book to Read
kidshealth.org/kid/grow/school_stuff/find_book.html
Find out how to choose good books at this site.

USA.gov—Book Report
https://www.usa.gov/book-report
Look here for tips on writing great book reports.

INDEX

About the AUTHORS

Cecilia Minden is the former director of the Language and Literacy Program at Harvard Graduate School of Education. She earned her doctorate from the University of Virginia. While at Harvard, Dr. Minden also taught several writing courses. Her research focused on early literacy skills and developing phonics curriculums. She is now a literacy consultant and the author of over 100 books for children. Dr. Minden lives with her family in McKinney, Texas. She enjoys helping students become interested in reading and writing.

Kate Roth has a doctorate from Harvard University in language and literacy and a master's degree from Columbia University Teachers College in curriculum and teaching. Her work focuses on writing instruction in the primary grades. She has taught kindergarten, first grade, and Reading Recovery. She has also instructed hundreds of teachers from around the world in early literacy practices. She lived with her husband and three children in China for many years, and now they live in Connecticut.